Rugby's FUNNIEST JOKES

Jim Chumley

summersdale

RUGBY'S FUNNIEST JOKES

Summersdale Publishers Ltd
46 West Street
Chichester
West Sussex
PO19 1RP
UK

www.summersdale.com

Printed and bound by Tien Wah Press

ISBN: 978-1-84024-746-6

Substantial discounts on bulk quantities of Summersdale books are available to corporations, professional associations and other organisations. For details telephone Summersdale Publishers on (+44-1243-771107), fax (+44-1243-786300) or email (nicky@summersdale.com).

Rugby's FUNNIEST JOKES

Jim Chumley

Editor's Note

Rugby is a notorious blood sport; a rough, tough, violent game with 15 players of whom, according to Jack Rowell, 'seven hate your guts and the other eight are making their minds up.' It is also a game ripe for comedy; how can it not be when it's a game played by men with odd-shaped balls?

This book will appeal to seasoned rugger buggers and young bloods alike – even armchair aficionados can find plenty of laughs to tackle in this veritable scrum of jokes and quotes. And, you might as well have a laugh during the game, for as the saying goes, 'in rugby there are no winners, only survivors.'

I Get a Kick Out of You

'Sorry I missed that conversion, captain,' said the player. 'I'm not sure what happened – it was such a simple shot. I could kick myself!'

'I wouldn't count on it,' replied the captain.

Two of the roughest rugby players were complaining about their coach's new tactics:

'It was much better in the past,' said one. 'All you had to remember was to kick ahead.'

'Yes,' said the other player, nodding in agreement.
'Any head would do!'

Did you hear about the new test for potential Worcester Warriors forwards?

They take them to Harrods for the first day of the January sale and if they manage to fight their way to the start of the queue, they're hired.

Why did the Irish rugby player
kick his opponent twice?

To be sure, to be sure.

'Rugby is a game for big buggers; if you're not a big bugger you get hurt. I wasn't a big bugger but I was a fast bugger and therefore avoided all the big buggers.'

SPIKE MILLIGAN

'If you can't take a punch,
you should play table tennis.'

FORMER FRENCH SKIPPER AND COACH PIERRE BERBIZIER
ILLUSTRATES HIS NATION'S ATTITUDE TO ON-PITCH VIOLENCE

A boy arrived home from
his rugby trial with a broken
finger, a cauliflower ear and
two wobbly teeth – but he
wasn't sure whose they were.

Pride of the Nation

'Of course it worries me if the All Blacks are invincible. I mean, it stands to reason – if we can't see them, how can we beat them?'

UNKNOWN ENGLISH RUGBY PLAYER

What do the Vultures have in common with a two pin plug?

Both are useless when you take them to Zimbabwe.

The coach took the Wallabies for a practice session. 'I want you all to get into your usual positions,' he said to his players. So they stood behind the goal and waited for the conversion.

What is the difference between the Azzurri and an arsonist?

An arsonist wouldn't waste six matches.

Practice was delayed for the US rugby squad when some white powder was found on the pitch. The coach reported this to the police and the powder was sent for analysis. Forensics managed to determine that the white powder was from the try line, and practice was resumed when the police concluded that it was unlikely that the team would ever come across this substance again.

What do you call 15 burly men huddled round the telly watching the Rugby World Cup Final?

The Spanish national team.

One Tongan rugby supporter
said to another:

'At one point I thought
we could actually win. But
then the game began...'

Why is it always so hot at a
Canadian national rugby match?

Because there's not a single
fan in the entire stadium.

Why Did the Rugby Player Cross the Pitch?

Why is it unwise to play
rugby on safari?

Because there's too many cheetahs.

Why was Cinderella
so bad at rugby?

She kept running away
from the ball.

'Waiter, waiter, why are there ears
in my soup?'
'It's OK, sir, they're cauliflower ears.'

Why do people tend to hate
Australian rugby players on sight?

Because it saves time.

Why do rugby players date
smart and beautiful women?

Because opposites attract.

Why don't rugby players
have mid-life crises?

Because they're stuck in adolescence.

Why couldn't the bicycle play in the rugby match?

Because it was two tyred.

All About England

What's the difference between
the English rugby team
and a box of Milk Tray?

You get better centres in
a box of chocolates.

'I've started going to
England rugby matches.'

'Why's that?'

'My doctor advised me I need
to avoid any excitement.'

What's the difference between
an English rugby player and
the PG Tips chimpanzee?

Some people can still remember
the PG Tips chimp holding a cup.

'They have this impression
of English rugby that
we all play in wellington
boots and we play in grass
that is two foot long.'

Sir Clive Woodward

'The only thing you're ever likely to catch on the end of an English back line is chilblains.'

DAVID CAMPESE

'Have you heard about the new English national team motto?'

'No, what's that?'

'"We'll win next time."'

The England fly half went up to his manager and said: 'I've got a great idea of how we could improve our game.' To which the manager replied: 'Brilliant! So when are you leaving?'

It was 'Bring your child to work day' for the English rugby team. Unfortunately, the children won 35-0.

'Giant gargoyles, raw-boned, cauliflower-eared monoliths that intimidated and unsettled. When they ran onto the field it was like watching a tribe of white orcs on steroids. Forget their hardness, has there ever been an uglier forward pack?'

MICHAEL LAWS ON ENGLAND'S WORLD CUP WINNING TEAM

Hit and Mrs

A rugby player's motto: Try during the day, but score at night.

A man was seated in the front row at a rugby World Cup match with an empty seat beside him. Another man saw the empty seat and asked him: 'Could I have this seat?'

'Of course you can,' replied the man. 'It was meant for my wife, but she died very recently.'

'Why didn't you invite anyone to come with you?' asked the man.

'They're all attending the funeral,' he replied.

Wife: Bob, you may be a good fly half, but you're a rubbish lover!

Husband: How are you able to tell in eight seconds?

'I once dated a famous
Aussie rugby player who
treated me just like a
football: made a pass, played
footsie, then dropped me
as soon as he'd scored.'

KATHY LETTE

A couple went to bed on their wedding night.

The new wife looked nervously at her husband and said, 'I have a confession to make: I was once a hooker.'

Her husband was very understanding, saying that the past was behind them.

She continued, 'There's something else... it used to be in the front row for the All Blacks.'

Why don't prop forwards
get Valentine's cards?

For religious reasons – God
made them ugly.

Just Blame the Ref

'Rule one: the referee is always right. Rule two: in the event of the referee being obviously wrong, rule one applies.'

PETER CORRIGAN

A rugby player approached the referee at the end of the match:

'My coach would like to know if there's a penalty for thinking.'

'No,' replied the ref.

'Well my captain thinks you're a prat, then,' said the player.

The rugby club disco was well under way when two people turned up demanding entry:

'You're not on the list, may I see your tickets?' asked the doorman.

'We don't have tickets,' said one. 'We're good mates with the ref.'

'Get going!' said the doorman. 'No ref I know has any mates.'

During a difficult match the
referee found himself being
heckled by one particular member
of the crowd. He turned a blind
eye, but when the heckler yelled,
'That was clearly a foul. Are you
blind, ref?', the referee marched
to the stands and shouted
angrily, 'What did you say?'
To which the spectator replied,
'Christ! Not only is he blind, but
he seems to be deaf as well!'

Why was the rugby referee mistaken for David Blaine?

He brought out so many cards that the crowd thought he must be a magician.

'I never wore a mouth
guard, hated them...
too uncomfortable and
besides, you couldn't
abuse the referee.'

CLIFF WATSON

What do rugby players do when
they start to lose their eyesight?

They become referees.

Two rugby referees went for a walk in the country. On their way they noticed some tracks. The first referee said, 'Are those motorbike tracks?' The second referee replied, 'No, they're definitely tractor tracks.' However, the conversation ended without warning when an express train hit them.

A referee went to his doctor to see why he was getting out of breath during his matches:

Doctor: Your problem is you're overweight.

Referee: I would like a second opinion.

Doctor: OK... You're ugly *and* you smell.

'You played an awful game today!' shouted the coach to his prop. 'You need more training.'

'What do you mean?' replied the prop. 'I've trained like Tarzan all week!'

'Maybe,' replied the coach. 'But you played like bloody Jane.'

You Know Your Rugby
Team's Bad When...

'I feel like I am the
captain of the *Titanic*.'

DAVE WATERSON, AFTER THE NAMIBIAN TEAM LOST 142–0
TO AUSTRALIA IN THE 2003 WORLD CUP

A couple had moved to a hut in the Himalayas to escape from the hustle and bustle of life.

'My rugby team lost their match today,' said the husband sadly.

'How on earth do you know that?' asked his wife.

'It's a Saturday.'

The Dream Team

Why is a successful rugby
team like a lingerie shop?

It has a wide variety of cups
and plenty of support.

The half-time score between England and the All Blacks was 30–0, with Jonah Lomu scoring six tries. Rather than playing the second half, the All Blacks decided to leave Jonah to finish the match single-handedly. At the final whistle, Jonah made his way to the pub to join his teammates with the final score being 60–3.

'How could you let them get three points??!' asked an angry teammate.

'I was sent off with ten minutes to go!' replied Jonah.

A journalist went to interview a scrum half in hospital after his game:

'Would you say you were the victim of a late tackle?' asked the journalist.

'You could call it that,' replied the scrum half. 'He punched me in the pub after the match.'

The winger had a bad day, dropping every ball that was passed to him. What's more, he felt a bit under the weather. 'I've got a cold coming on,' he muttered.

'Well, it makes a change that you've been able to catch something,' grumbled the scrum half.

'We've lost seven of our
last eight matches. Only
team that we've beaten
was Western Samoa.
Good job we didn't play
the whole of Samoa.'

GARETH DAVIES

'You have fifteen players
in a team. Seven hate your
guts and the other eight are
making their minds up.'

JACK ROWELL

'What position do you
play in the team?'

'Back.'

'Which one?'

'The drawback.'

Fred had always played rugby in the Sunday league. This troubled his wife, so she asked the vicar whether it was a sin to play on Sunday.

'It's not a sin,' replied the vicar. 'The way he plays, it's a *crime!*'

'[Rugby is] a game played by fewer than fifteen a side, at least half of whom should be totally unfit.'

MICHAEL GREEN

'This is the deal,' said the rugby manager. '£5,000 a month now, £8,000 a month in two years.'

'Great,' replied the prop. 'I'll see you in two years, then.'

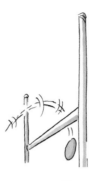

Brain vs Brawn

'Nobody in rugby should be called a genius. A genius is a guy like Norman Einstein.'

JONO GIBBES

A rugby coach walked into the changing room before a big match and went up to his latest signing:

Coach: I've been told that I can't allow you to play until you've mastered simple arithmetic. Could you tell me what one plus two makes?

New player: Is it three, sir?

The team shouted together: Give him another chance!

The team's manager, coach, fullback and winger are flying to the cup final when the plane's engines die.

The coach says, 'There are only three parachutes! The squad needs me – I'm taking one,' and jumps.

The winger says, 'I'm the cleverest man on the team – I'm taking one,' and jumps.

The manager says to the fullback, 'The last parachute is yours.' 'We can both have one,' he replies. 'The cleverest man on the team jumped with my kit bag on his back.'

Things weren't going too well for the home team so the coach shouted to his star prop, 'You've got to fight, son, get in there!' So the prop fought his way across the field and knocked out the referee.

'Rugby players are like lava lamps: good to look at but not very bright.'

UNKNOWN

What did the coach say to the super-sized, super-slow rugby player?

'Get moving! You're killing the turf!'

The winger was clouted in the head during a tackle and knocked out cold. As the paramedic waved a towel at him and sprayed water on his face to revive him, he came round.

'Bloody hell,' he exclaimed. 'It was sunny when I fell over; this wind and rain's come from nowhere.'

Injury Time

'Sure there have been injuries
and deaths in rugby – but
none of them serious.'

JOHN 'DOC' MAYHEW

Why do rugby players wear numbers on their jerseys?

Because the coroner can't always identify their bodies by their dental records alone.

A man arrived for work on Monday with a broken arm and a dislocated knee:

'The Six Nations Cup result wasn't what I hoped it would be... and now my TV is broken.'

A rugby player visited his doctor:

'Doctor, doctor, every morning when I look at myself in the mirror, I feel like being sick. What could be wrong with me?'

'I don't know,' the doctor replied after inspecting his eyes. 'But your vision is perfect!'

A rugby player went to his doctor with an injury: 'When I finished playing the match, I touched my stomach, my forehead, my legs and everything really hurts.'

The doctor examined him and replied, 'You've fractured your finger.'

'How is your husband?'

'He's at home with a rugby injury.'

'You didn't tell me he played rugby.'

'Oh, he doesn't – he just strained
his larynx at the game last week.'

'In rugby there are no winners, only survivors.'

UNKNOWN

Have you enjoyed this book? If so, why not write a review on your favourite website? Thanks very much for buying this Summersdale book.

www.summersdale.com